Scholastic Canada Biographies

CANADIAN EXPLORERS

Maxine Trottier

illustrated by

Tony Meers

Scholastic Canada Ltd.

Toronto New York London Auckland Sydney
Mexico City New Delhi Hong Kong Buenos Aires

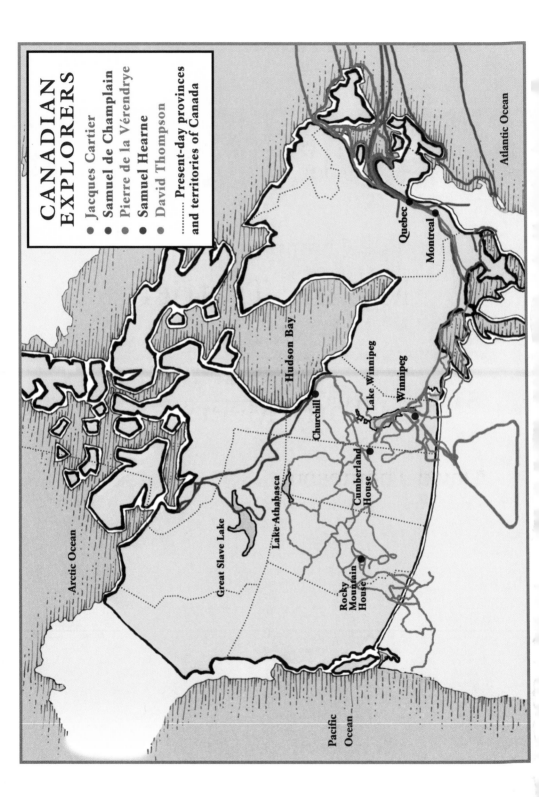

CANADIAN
EXPLORERS

- Jacques Cartier
- Samuel de Champlain
- Pierre de la Vérendrye
- Samuel Hearne
- David Thompson
······· Present-day provinces
and territories of Canada

Arctic Ocean

Great Slave Lake

Lake Athabasca

Rocky
Mountain
House

Pacific
Ocean

Churchill

Cumberland
House

Hudson Bay

Lake Winnipeg

Winnipeg

Quebec

Montreal

Atlantic Ocean

Contents

Jacques Cartier
Up the St. Lawrence River

At one time people believed that China and its riches could be reached by sailing west across the Atlantic Ocean. It was simply a matter of finding a passage through the New World. In 1534 Jacques Cartier set out to do just that.

Jacques, the second child of Jamet Cartier and Geseline Jansart, was born in 1491 at St. Malo, France. Destined to go to sea, he studied navigation. Years later, when King François I ordered Jacques to ". . . discover certain islands and countries where it is said that a great abundance of gold and other precious things is to be found," he was ready.

On April 20, 1534, Jacques Cartier set sail from

St. Malo with two ships and 61 men, leaving his wife, Catherine, behind. Twenty days later, after an amazingly quick voyage, they had crossed the Atlantic. For weeks Cartier explored what would later be called Newfoundland, the Magdalen Islands, Prince Edward Island – and the Gaspé Peninsula. There Micmacs offered the strangers animal skins in exchange for knives, iron goods and a red hat for their chief. The fur trade in the New World had begun.

On July 24 Cartier had his men build a nine-metre cross and set it into the ground on the Gaspé. There he took possession of the country for his king. More than 200 Iroquois fishing nearby witnessed the event. Their chief, Donnacona, was not pleased.

When Cartier and his men returned to their ships, Donnacona, three of his sons and his brother

followed in a canoe. Cartier forced them to come aboard, and assured Donnacona that the cross was only a landmark to lead them back. He also asked the chief to allow two of his sons, Domagaya and Taignoagny, to return to France with him. They could learn French and act as interpreters. Donnacona agreed.

The expedition was back in St. Malo that September. Ordered by the king to continue exploring, Cartier left France again on May 19,

This map made by Pierre Desceliers in 1550 uses the word CANADA.

1535, with three ships and 110 men. This time the voyage was a long one of 50 days with much bad weather. The *Petite Hermine*, the *Émérillon* and Cartier's flagship, the *Grande Hermine*, became separated. As agreed, they met off the coast of Newfoundland.

With the guidance of Domagaya and Taignoagny, the ships sailed into the Gulf of St. Lawrence and up the St. Lawrence River. The young Iroquois, who now spoke some French, had told Cartier many things about their home, referring to it as *kanata,* which means "the village." Cartier, misunderstanding what they had said, began to call the entire area Canada, a name that by 1547 was being used on maps.

When the explorers arrived at the Iroquois village of Stadacona, where Quebec City now stands, Donnacona and the almost 2000 people living there greeted them warmly.

That fall Cartier journeyed upriver to Hochelaga, the site of Montreal. There he saw the Iroquois smoking dried leaves in their pipes. It was tobacco.

Back at Stadacona for the winter, Cartier's men built a small fort, and harsh weather set in. The men began to fall ill with scurvy, a disease caused by a lack of vitamin C. Questioning Domagaya, Cartier learned how to use the bark and needles of the *annedda* (white cedar) to brew a drink. Unaware that the drink contained vitamin C, Cartier only knew that it helped. Twenty-five men died, but the rest survived.

In the spring of 1536, his crew no longer big

enough to handle three ships, Cartier abandoned the *Petite Hermine*. He then seized Donnacona, his two French-speaking sons and seven other Iroquois, including four children. Even though Cartier vowed to bring back their chief in a year, Donnacona's people were very upset.

Back in France, though, it wasn't until the fall of 1540 – more than four years later – that Jacques Cartier had a third commission from the king. This time he would be under the command of Jean-François de la Roque de Roberval. But Roberval was so slow in readying his ships that, in May of 1541, Cartier was finally given permission to set out.

He returned to Stadacona with five ships and 1500 men. When asked by the Iroquois about the whereabouts of Donnacona, Cartier admitted that their leader was dead. He told them that the others were well and being treated like royalty in France. The truth was that all but one little girl had died.

The friendliness of the people of Stadacona ended. Unwelcome there, Cartier went upriver to establish a settlement at the base of Cap Rouge that he called Charlesbourg Royal. He wrote that "the country is as fit for cultivation as one could find or desire." He found what he believed to be gold and diamonds, but they were not enough to keep him there. Because of the hostility – 35 of his men were killed by the Iroquois – Cartier abandoned the settlement in the spring of 1542, deciding to return to France. He met with Roberval's ship near Newfoundland, but he refused to turn back. Disobeying orders, he continued on his way.

The treasures that Cartier brought home turned out to be worthless pyrite and quartz. With his days of exploration over, he became a successful businessman. He died at Limoelou, his home near St. Malo, on the morning of September 1, 1557.

Cartier had voyaged 1600 kilometres up the St. Lawrence River – the first known European to do so. Although it did not last, he had established the first French settlement in Canada. His explorations marked the beginning of hundreds of years of France's influence here. Last but not least, Jacques Cartier gave our country its name.

Today Jacques Cartier's home near St. Malo, France, is a museum.

Samuel de Champlain
In the Heart of New France

Little is known about Samuel de Champlain's early years. The son of Margueritte Le Roy and Anthoine de Complain, a sea captain, he was born at Brouage, France, between 1567 and 1570. The exact date remains a mystery, since the church records were destroyed by fire.

Samuel went to sea with his uncle and voyaged to Spain, enjoying navigation from a young age. The drawing, map-making and navigating skills he learned led to a lifelong adventure. He was offered the chance to sail to the New World with François Gravé Du Pont on a trading expedition. The adventure had begun.

In 1603 Samuel de Champlain boarded the *Bonne Renommée*, one of three ships that set sail from Honfleur, France, on March 15. After a long voyage peppered with storms, fog and icebergs, they had crossed the Atlantic and entered the St. Lawrence River.

When the expedition arrived at Tadoussac in late May, the Algonquin people living there held a *tabagie,* or feast. Men ran races for prizes and the women danced. Champlain tasted beaver, seal blubber and moose meat for the first time. While the others traded, Champlain went 12 leagues (about 50 kilometres) up the Saguenay River with some Algonquins in birchbark canoes.

In mid-June the expedition continued up the St. Lawrence River, reaching a place the Algonquins

Map of New France made by Champlain in 1612

called *kebec,* meaning "where the river narrows." Champlain wrote, ". . . in my opinion, if this soil were tilled, it would be as good as ours."

Back in France that fall, Champlain presented a map of the St. Lawrence River to the king. The next spring Champlain left for Acadia, now called Nova Scotia, on a ship commanded by Pierre Du Gua de Monts. This time Champlain was the expedition's geographer and map-maker.

From 1604 to 1607, settlements were built at the island of St. Croix and then at Port Royal. To raise the men's spirits during the first long winter at Port Royal, Champlain founded the Order of Good Cheer. Each member, wearing a ceremonial chain, took a turn providing a meal of game or fish. Champlain wrote that everyone found it "beneficial to his health, and more profitable than all sorts of medicine we might have used." During his years at Port Royal, Champlain explored the coast for about 1500 kilometres, from Cape Breton to Cape Cod, and drew maps.

The king of France was being pressured by rival fur traders, so in 1607 the colony lost its trading privilege and Champlain and the others returned to France. There he became part of another expedition, this time as a lieutenant under de Monts. Their ship, the *Don de Dieu,* arrived at Tadoussac on June 3, 1608. Leaving the ship behind, Champlain took a party of 24 men up the river in a smaller boat called a barque. His destination was Quebec.

There they began to fell trees. He wrote, "I at once employed a part of our workmen in cutting them down to make a site for our settlement, another part in sawing planks, another in digging the cellar and making ditches." They constructed three main buildings and a storehouse, all surrounded by stockades and moats. This was Champlain's Habitation.

Champlain's engraving of the Habitation, 1608

For the next 20 years, Champlain and his companions struggled to keep the settlement and themselves alive. They battled scurvy and harsh weather. He allied himself with the Hurons, the Algonquins and the Montagnais, who not only

came to the Habitation to trade but who accompanied him on further explorations.

It was on one such journey to the west that Samuel de Champlain saw a lake that he named Lake Champlain. There his party came upon a large group of Iroquois. In the battle that followed, Champlain shot two of the Iroquois chiefs with his harquebus, killing them.

In 1610, while in France, Champlain had married 12-year-old Hélène Boullé, gaining her dowry of 6000 *livres*. According to the marriage contract, Hélène would live with her parents until she was 14, but it was not until 1620 that Champlain brought her to the Habitation. She stayed only four years and then returned with him to France.

Samuel de Champlain was back in Quebec by 1626, without Hélène. Wanting a family, he decided to adopt some children. The Montagnais offered him three girls, aged 11, 12 and 15. Champlain gave them the names Foi, Espérance and Charité (Faith, Hope and Charity). Foi soon returned to her people, but Champlain provided the other two girls with a French education, including how "to use a needle, both for making clothes and for embroidering."

Unfortunately his family life was not to last. On September 14, 1629, the Kirke brothers, Louis and Thomas, attacked Quebec and seized it in the name of England. Forcing Champlain to sail back to France, they refused to let him take his daughters. He never saw them again.

It was not until 1632 that France and England signed the Treaty of St. Germain en Laye, which

returned ownership of Canada to France. The next year Champlain and almost 200 settlers in three ships arrived at Quebec. With their help he rebuilt the ruins of the Habitation and enlarged the fortifications with "new courage." He died there on Christmas Day, 1635.

Samuel de Champlain, the Father of New France, successfully forged trading and military agreements with the Native peoples. He was strong and determined enough to criss-cross the ocean 21 times and spend years in the wilderness, and even shot the Lachine Rapids in a canoe. By instructing

Espérance and Charité, he sowed the seeds of French education at Quebec. His published journals, filled with maps, charts and detailed drawings, let us see Canada through the eyes of a dedicated colonist and explorer. Because of Champlain's tireless work, New France would continue to grow.

Champlain's astrolabe, dated 1605

A statue of Champlain surveys Lake Couchiching at Orillia, Ontario.

The title page of Champlain's 1632 journal

Pierre de la Vérendrye

Westward to Winnipeg

In 1685, the town of Trois Rivières on the St. Lawrence River was a small trading post enclosed by a stone palisade. It was the home of René Gaultier de Varennes et de la Vérendrye, his wife Marie Boucher and their 12 children. On November 17 of that year, one more was added to the family when their son Pierre was born.

At the age of 11, Pierre was sent to study at the Jesuit Seminary in Quebec. Three years later he joined the army. Between 1704 and 1705, he fought the British in New England and Newfoundland, first as a cadet and then as an ensign.

Since his eldest brother Louis had died, Pierre adopted his title of La Vérendrye. Anxious to rise in rank, he left behind his fiancée, Marie-Anne Dandonneau Du Sablé, and sailed to France. There he joined the Régiment de Bretagne and was made a lieutenant. He was seriously wounded in battle by a musket ball and eight sword thrusts, and was taken prisoner for four months.

Unable to afford the life of an officer, Pierre de la Vérendrye returned to New France in 1712 and married Marie-Anne. They settled down at their farm on Île aux Vaches near Trois Rivières, where their six children were born. But by the age of 40, La Vérendrye believed that his life of farming and a little fur trading had been unsuccessful. So in 1726 he voyaged west and joined his brother Jacques-René at Kaministiquia (Thunder Bay). He became Jacques-René's second-in-command at the trading post, and when his brother left, he took over his responsibilities.

Since the time of Cartier, people had believed that there must be a large gulf, or Western Sea, by which they could reach the Pacific Ocean and China. La Vérendrye had questioned many of the Native people who came to the post. They told him tales of river systems and a place called Lake Ouinipigon (Lake Winnipeg). One man, a Cree named Auchagah, even drew him a map using charcoal.

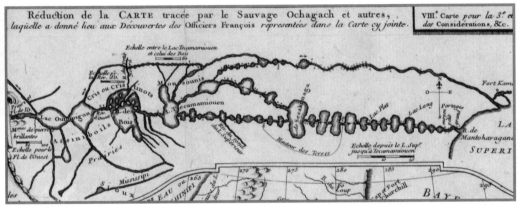

A map drawn by Auchagah for La Vérendrye

Convinced that this must be the route to the Western Sea, La Vérendrye returned to Quebec in 1730 and met with the governor. The officials decided to send him west the next spring to build a trading post on Lake Ouinipigon. He was given only 2000 *livres* with which to buy gifts for the Native peoples he would meet. This meant that La Vérendrye had to seek financial support, so he formed a partnership with nine merchants.

On June 8, 1731, La Vérendrye set out from Montreal with his sons François, Jean-Baptiste and Pierre, his nephew and 50 *engagés* (hired men). Auchagah agreed to accompany them as their guide.

La Vérendrye wrote, "With reference to the guide, the man I have chosen is one named Auchagah, a savage of my post, greatly attached to the French nation, the man most capable of guiding a party, and with whom there would be no fear of our being abandoned on the way."

During the next years, La Vérendrye would travel thousands of kilometres, exploring the wilderness on foot and by canoe. Mild-mannered and dedicated, he built eight trading posts, including one called Fort La Reine. La Vérendrye was not only sending back furs, he was also sending Native slaves to New France. It was a difficult existence, sometimes touched by tragedy. His nephew became ill and died. In the spring of 1736, Jean-Baptiste and a party of men were ambushed

and killed by Sioux warriors while they were on their way to Michilimackinac for supplies.

La Vérendrye's business partners took over his trading posts in 1735 so that he could devote himself to exploration. He had long heard mysterious stories of the Mandans, people with light skin and hair and blue eyes who might know the route to the Western Sea. He decided to find them. On September 28, 1738, he reached the mouth of the Assiniboine River, where Winnipeg now stands. The next month, with about four dozen men, including his sons Louis-Joseph and François and 25 Assiniboines, La Vérendrye set out. Early in December, he entered the main Mandan village on the Missouri River. To his frustration the people there knew of no route.

Two years later, back in Montreal, La Vérendrye learned that his wife was dead and buried. Returning to Fort La Reine, eager to continue exploring, he found he no longer had the stamina. By this time it was 1742 and he was 57 years old. Instead, he sent Louis-Joseph and François west. His sons and their party journeyed as far as what they described as "the shining mountains," which were probably the Big Horn Mountains in Wyoming.

La Vérendrye returned to Montreal for the last time in 1744, where, for a while, he gave up his dream of exploration. He entertained friends and even courted a wife. He was awarded the Cross of St. Louis, a great honour, and was planning yet another expedition when he died on December 5, 1749.

More than 160 years later, on a hill overlooking Fort Pierre, South Dakota, some schoolchildren found a lead tablet. On it was the name of the man whose sons had buried it there for their father: Pierre Gaultier de la Vérendrye.

At an age when others might have been retiring, Pierre had ventured out as an explorer. He and his sons went farther west than any other known Canadians of the time. Because of the chain of trading posts he built, the river of furs that had once flowed only to the Hudson's Bay Company would now go to Montreal as well. Through his exploration Pierre de la Vérendrye had opened the west to the French.

A monument overlooking Fort Pierre, South Dakota, honours the La Vérendryes.

The lead tablet that was buried in South Dakota, showing the inscriptions on both sides

Samuel Hearne
Across the Barren Lands

Samuel Hearne, the son of Diana and Samuel, was born in London, England, in 1745. When his father died three years later, his mother moved Samuel and his sister to the village of Beaminster. With this journey of a few hundred kilometres, Samuel's life of travel and exploration began.

At the age of 11, Samuel joined the Royal Navy as a captain's servant. After much action at sea during the Seven Years War, in 1763 Samuel left the navy. Three years later he joined the Hudson's Bay Company in London, England, and crossed the Atlantic Ocean for the first time. He acted as mate on the *Charlotte*, a ship that carried on fur trading

between the Inuit and Prince of Wales Fort on Hudson Bay.

The chief factor, or commander, of the fort, Moses Norton, had heard of vast mineral riches in the far north. Copper nuggets had been brought in, and more discoveries could lure new trading partners to the fort. He authorized an expedition, and Samuel Hearne was chosen to lead it.

The first two expeditions, in 1769 and 1770, ended in failure because of Norton's poor choices in guides. Hearne was abandoned on the first trip. On the second he was robbed and became lost.

Refusing to let Norton select a guide for his next attempt, Hearne chose a Chipewyan man named Matonabbee. In Matonabbee's opinion the expeditions had failed because Hearne had not brought along women. He said that, "Women were made for labour; one of them can carry, or haul, as

much as two men can do." They would also pitch the tents and make and mend clothing. Hearne agreed and attached himself to what he called Matonabbee's gang, which included a number of men as well as Matonabbee's six wives and their children.

They set out to cross the Barren Lands on December 7, 1770. The heavy pack Hearne carried was made awkward by his navigational instruments. His tent and clothing were often wet, and snowstorms struck without warning. Hearne had to eat what the others did. He became used to raw muskox meat and caribou stomach, but he could not bring himself to eat the lice that Matonabbee so enjoyed.

For the sake of speed, that summer the women and children were left behind in a camp. On July 14, 1771, Hearne and the men arrived at the

Coppermine River only to find it so shallow in spots that the company's ships would never be able to use it. It was there that they came upon a group of Inuit. Hearne was unable to prevent Matonabbee and his men from slaughtering them all. In memory of this horrible event, he named the spot Bloody Fall.

Three days later Samuel Hearne reached the Arctic Ocean and took possession of the coast on behalf of the Hudson's Bay Company. Following the Coppermine River on the return journey, he did find copper 48 kilometres from the river's mouth. He brought back a 2-kilogram chunk.

In the great rush to get back to the women and children, the pace was doubled. Hearne's toenails became infected and some of them fell off. However, once back with their families, the Chipewyans were in no hurry to return to the fort

on Hudson Bay. More and more people joined the expedition until there were hundreds travelling with Hearne. They could only make 10 to 12 kilometres a day.

After wintering in the forest, the party arrived back at the fort in July. Hearne had been gone more than one and a half years and had walked more than 5600 kilometres – the first known Englishman to reach the Arctic Ocean on foot and to walk across an enormous frozen body of water, Athapuscow Lake (now called Great Slave Lake). He wrote, "My discoveries are not likely to prove of any material advantage to the Nation at large, or indeed to the Hudson's Bay Company, yet I have the pleasure to think that I have fully complied with the orders of my Masters." In spite of his modesty, Hearne's journey had been exceptional. So were the writings and drawings he had done.

Hearne once again served on the *Charlotte*, but by 1773, word of his journals had reached company headquarters in London. He was chosen to found the company's first inland post. This he built the next year in what is now Saskatchewan, and called it Cumberland House. Hearne would have carried on there, but in 1775 the company appointed him governor of Prince of Wales Fort.

In 1782, during the American Revolution, three French warships allied to the Americans arrived in Hudson Bay. Many of the Native people escaped into the woods, and Hearne surrendered the fort. He watched helplessly as the French blew up it up. Hearne and the other prisoners were allowed to sail back to England in a small ship.

The next year he returned to the ruins to find that Matonabbee, thinking him dead, had hanged himself in despair. Smallpox had killed many of the Native people and the rest had moved away. Nearby,

The restored Prince of Wales Fort is a National Historic Site.

Hearne dutifully built a small wooden house, "Fort Churchill," and carried on until his health began to fail. He retired in 1787 and returned to London.

Although people would continue to search for riches, and for a Northwest Passage to the Orient, Samuel Hearne had proved that there was no short route to either. His explorations were a success because he adapted so well to the lifestyle of the Native peoples. *A Journey from Prince of Wales's Fort, in Hudson's Bay, to the Northern Ocean,* his account of his adventures, was published three years after his death in 1792 in London. Its detailed drawings and careful observations describe an amazing tale of survival. Samuel Hearne, a keen observer of nature and people, remains an outstanding explorer of Canada's north.

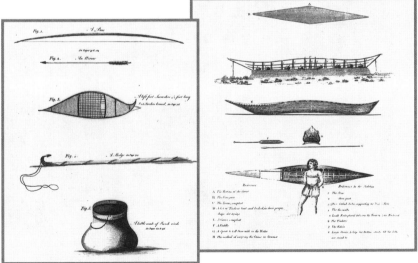

Samuel Hearne drew these Native implements – a bow, an arrow, a snowshoe, a sledge, a kettle and a canoe (various views) – on his expeditions.

David Thompson
From Hudson Bay to the Pacific

David Thompson, named after his father, came into the world on April 30, 1770, in London, England. When his father died two years later, David and his mother and baby brother were left with very little. David was sent to The Grey Coat Hospital, a charity school for poor children near Westminster Abbey. From that time on, he seldom had contact with his family.

David had a talent for mathematics, so he studied navigation with the idea of having a career in the navy. Then the Hudson's Bay Company made a request to the school for boys to work in the fur trade in Canada. David was a likely choice. At the age of 14, he was apprenticed to the company for seven years.

David's first year was spent under the direction of Samuel Hearne at Fort Churchill on Hudson Bay. Among other things, he was assigned the job of copying out parts of Hearne's manuscript, *A Journey from Prince of Wales's Fort, in Hudson's Bay, to the Northern Ocean.* When he wasn't working, David observed seals, polar bears and birds. He even studied mosquitoes under a microscope.

It was an adventurous life. When he was 15, David was given the job of delivering mail to York Factory. He made the 240-kilometre journey with only two Native guides. David worked at many different forts and learned to speak Peigan and Cree.

Two days before Christmas in 1788, at the fort called Manchester House, David broke his leg in a sled accident. The bad break healed slowly, and in the spring he was carried to Cumberland House. By summer he was on crutches.

A surveying party led by a man named Peter Turnor had arrived at Cumberland House. Turnor was to survey the Athabasca country to the west. That winter David studied astronomy, surveying and mathematics under Turnor. But not only was he still not strong enough for the expedition that spring, David had become blind in one eye. He wrote, "By too much attention to calculations in the night, with no other light than a small candle my right eye became so inflamed that I lost its sight."

David Thompson returned to York Factory to complete his apprenticeship. Successful, he wrote to the company and asked for a sextant and other surveying tools, instead of the suit of clothes given on the occasion. Recognizing his ability, not only did they send the tools, they offered him a contract and a wage of 15 pounds a year.

Thompson surveyed the country between the Nelson and Churchill Rivers, and found a new route to Lake Athabasca for the company. By 1797, although he was working as a surveyor making 60 pounds a year, he wanted to devote himself to map-making. He joined the North West Company, the Hudson's Bay Company's rival. While working for them he met Charlotte Small, a 13-year-old Métis

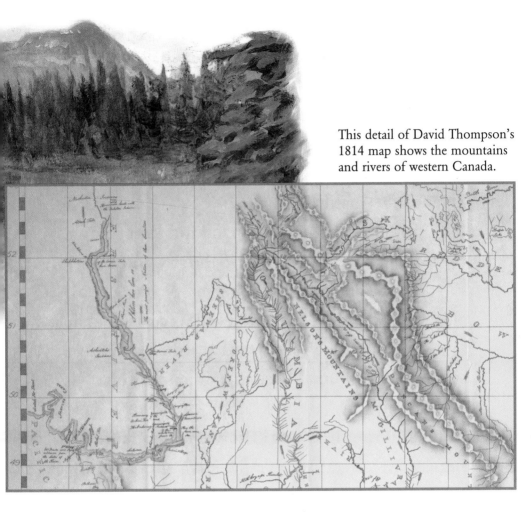

This detail of David Thompson's 1814 map shows the mountains and rivers of western Canada.

girl. Later he would write, "On June 10th Charlotte became my wife and many a mile and river we have travelled together since."

David Thompson and Charlotte moved to Rocky Mountain House. During the next 15 years he explored and mapped the mountains, often with Charlotte and their growing family in tow. He surveyed the Peace River, crossed the Rocky Mountains using the Howse Pass and established a trading post that he named Kootenai House.

He explored the Spokane and Kootenay Rivers and built trading posts in what are now British Columbia and the states of Idaho, Washington and Montana. Crossing the Rockies by way of the Athabasca Pass, he travelled down the Columbia River to the Pacific Ocean.

All the while he drew maps and kept journals. He told about eating beaver tail, lynx and buffalo. He described dozens of different Native peoples, once writing that he had always admired their ability to ". . . guide themselves through the darkest pine forests to exactly the place they intended to go."

Thompson retired from the North West Company in 1812 and moved his family to Terrebonne, near Montreal. His wife and their children were baptized. He and Charlotte exchanged formal wedding vows that October and he began redrawing his maps, hoping to have them published as an atlas. He eventually moved his family to Glengarry County, Ontario, where for 10 years he worked for the Boundary Commission, surveying the border between the United States and Canada.

By 1843 David Thompson's atlas was finally completed. He had mapped an area of 3.9 million square kilometres stretching from Hudson Bay to the Pacific. By this point David and Charlotte were so poor that they had to move in with one of their daughters. Several times he had to pawn his surveying instruments, and once his coat. He began to write an account of his travels from his 77 original journals, but when he became entirely blind, it remained unfinished.

David Thompson died on February 10, 1857, his passing unnoticed by the public. Charlotte followed him three months later. They had been married for 57 years and had raised a family of 13 children.

It was not until 1916 that *David Thompson's Narrative* was published by The Champlain Society. A person of great integrity, Thompson had never once traded whisky for furs. Because he was always gazing into the night sky with his sextant so that he could calculate latitude and longitude, the Native people had given him a nickname. It was *Koo-koo-sint,* or "the man who looks at stars." A writer, a naturalist, an explorer and a map-maker, David Thompson is considered to be one of the world's greatest land geographers.

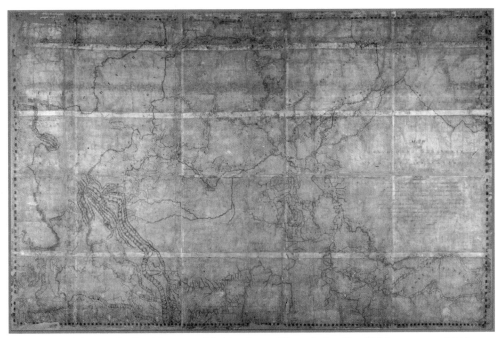

Map of the North-West Territory of the Province of Canada by David Thompson, 1814
Today the original is on display at the Ontario Archives.

THE
PUBLICATIONS OF
THE CHAMPLAIN
SOCIETY

DAVID THOMPSON'S NARRATIVE
1784-1812

TORONTO
THE CHAMPLAIN SOCIETY

The title page of David
Thompson's journal

For my niece, Erin Willner
— M.T.

Photo Credits

Page 6: Pierre Desceliers, Library and Archives Canada NMC-0009897
Page 9: Courtesy of Le Musée Stewart
Page 13: Samuel de Champlain, Carte géographique de la Nouvelle Franse faictte par le sieur de Champlain Saint Tongois [Saintongeois] cappitaine ordinaire pur le Roy et la Marine, Library and Archives Canada C-118494
Page 15: Samuel de Champlain, Habitation de Québec, Library and Archives Canada C-009711
Page 19: (left) Courtesy of Joan Woodrow; (upper right) Champlain's astrolabe dated 1605, Library and Archives Canada C-008336; (lower right) Title page of Champlain's 1632 account "Les voyages de la Nouvelle France occidentale, dicte Canada faits par le s' de Champlain," Library and Archives Canada, from transparency
Page 23: Map drawn by native Auchagah, Library and Archives Canada NMC-13295
Page 27: Photos courtesy of the South Dakota State Historical Society – State Archives
Page 34: © Parks Canada/Bill, R.E. – 1977, H.07.72.02.06 (27)
Page 35: Hudson's Bay Company Archives, Archives of Manitoba, HBCA Library: (left) RB FC 3212.2 H4 Plate III (N7926); (right) RB FC 3212.2 H4 Plate V (N15162)
Page 41: Detail from Map of the North-West Territory of the Province of Canada, from David Thompson's Narrative 1784-1812, The Champlain Society
Page 45: (upper) David Thompson, Map of the North-West Territory of the Province of Canada, Archives of Ontario, David Thompson fonds, F 443, R-C (U), AO 1541; (lower) Title page of David Thompson's narrative, Library and Archives Canada NLC-000724

Canadian Explorers route map by Paul Dotey and Yüksel Hassan

Library and Archives Canada Cataloguing in Publication

Trottier, Maxine
Canadian explorers / Maxine Trottier ; Tony Meers, illustrator.

(Scholastic Canada biographies)
ISBN 0-439-96170-X

1. Explorers—Canada—Biography—Juvenile literature.
2. Canada—Discovery and exploration—Juvenile literature.
I. Meers, Tony II. Title. III. Series.

FC172 .T76 2005   j917.104'092'2   C2004-904277-7

6 5 4   Printed in Canada   119   10 11 12 13